Adelaide

This book belongs to

Grandma

Given with love from

2018

Happy Easter

Happy Birthday

Note to Grandparents

**"THERE'S NOTHING MORE WONDERFUL
THAN BEING A GRANDPARENT!"**

I'll admit I was skeptical the first time I heard those words.
But when our daughter placed her beautiful little newborn girl
into my arms for the very first time, I found out something you've
known for quite a while—*they were absolutely right!* What a joy
to relive those wonderful days. And what a gift to have another
chance to slow down, snuggle up, and share God's amazing love
with a whole new generation of precious little ones.

Enjoy!

Phil A. Smouse

My Time with Grandma
Bible Storybook

Written by Phil A. Smouse Illustrated by Ela Jarzabek

TYNDALE KIDS

Tyndale House Publishers, Inc.
Carol Stream, Illinois

God Is Our Father

GENESIS 1:1-27

In the beginning God made the heavens and the earth.

On the first day, he said, "Let there be light!"
On the second day, he hung the clouds in the sky.
On the third day, his hands formed the land and the sea.
On the fourth day, he painted the night with stars.
On the fifth day, he made each bird and fish.
On the sixth day, he made every animal that cuddles or crawls.

God looked at the world. He saw it was good.
So from the good earth, he made a man.
And with the man, a woman.
Both were made in the image of God—his very own children—
Adam and Eve!

Love Note from Grandma

God made the sun and the moon. He made the earth and the stars. He made the plants and the animals and every good thing. But God knew something was missing. So he made the most wonderful thing of all. Do you know what it is? That's right—he made you!

Love Note from God

You are God's child.

Galatians 4:7

3

Our Father Knows Best

GENESIS 2:15-17; 3:1-23

God placed Adam and Eve in a beautiful garden. He gave them everything they could ever want. And they were happy. "Now remember," God said, "do not eat fruit from the tree in the center of the Garden." So Adam and Eve did just as God said.

But the devil hated Adam and Eve. He hated God and the beautiful world God had made. So he became a snake. He tricked Adam and Eve. They ate fruit from the tree! Oh no! Now they would have to leave God's wonderful Garden—*forever!*

Love Note from Grandma

God knows what's best for us. He knows what will hurt us too. When God says "no," he's not trying to be grumpy or mean. And he's not trying to stop us from having fun. He's trying to make sure we are safe, happy, and close to him forever.

Love Note from God

The Lord corrects those he loves.

Proverbs 3:12

God Keeps Us Safe

GENESIS 6:9-22

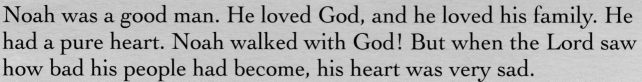

Noah was a good man. He loved God, and he loved his family. He had a pure heart. Noah walked with God! But when the Lord saw how bad his people had become, his heart was very sad.

So God said to Noah, "I am going to bring a great flood upon the earth! It will rain for forty days and forty nights. Build a big boat out of wood. Take your family into the boat. Bring along two of every kind of animal. Keep them all safe and alive during the flood."

So Noah did everything exactly as God said.

Love Note from Grandma

I love you so much. But God loves you even more! And he wants you to trust him. When you're at home, in the car, or even outside playing, God is watching over you. God kept Noah safe. He will make sure you are safe too.

6

Love Note from God

**You protect me
from my troubles.**

Psalm 32:7

7

God Says, "Don't Be Afraid!"

1 SAMUEL 17:1-50

The army of God was very afraid. Their enemy Goliath was over nine feet tall. "Come out and fight!" the giant roared. But nobody moved—until little David appeared.

David didn't have a sword—just a slingshot and five smooth stones. Was David afraid? No! Goliath was big, but God was bigger.

"Come and get it!" Goliath laughed as he moved closer and closer. But little David was ready. Out came his sling. In went the stone. *Bop!* Goliath crashed to the ground before he even knew what hit him! God helped David beat the giant!

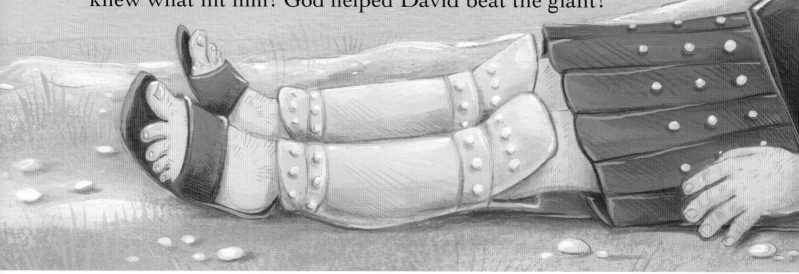

Love Note from Grandma

No problem is too big or too scary for God. So trust him and always do your best. You don't ever have to be afraid. With God's help, your little hands can do some very big things!

8

God Will Take Care of Us

1 KINGS 17:1-6

Ahab was a very bad king. He did many things that made God angry. But Elijah was not like Ahab. Elijah loved God. So God gave Elijah a message to take to the king.

"King Ahab!" Elijah cried. "Quit doing bad things, or the rain will stop!" Did the king listen? No! So Elijah prayed very hard for God to stop the rain. God answered Elijah's prayer. Soon the land was so dry, there was no food growing *anywhere!*

But God loved Elijah—and Elijah loved him. So God whispered, "Go past the Jordan River to the land of Kerith. You will be safe there. Drink from the brook. Every morning and evening, *look up!* The birds will bring you bread and meat to eat."

So the birds came just as God said. And Elijah ate his food with joy!

Love Note from Grandma

Our lives are like a big puzzle. Sometimes they look like a mess. And there always seems to be a piece missing somewhere. But Jesus knows what we need. When we put our lives in his hands *and give him all the pieces,* he will make something beautiful.

Love Note from God

Your heavenly Father will give good things to those who ask him.

Matthew 7:11

11

God Is Always with Us

DANIEL 3:1-27

The king was very angry! Shadrach, Meshach, and Abednego would not bow down and worship his golden statue. "Build a fire, and make it seven times hotter than usual," the king ordered. "Then throw them in!" So the three men were tied up and thrown into the fire.

The king leaped to his feet and looked in. "Didn't we throw three men into the furnace? Now there are four. And one of them looks like the Son of God! Come out! Come out!" the king cried. So out they came. Their clothes were not burned. Their hair wasn't either. They didn't even smell like smoke. God saved them from the fire!

Love Note from Grandma

Some days are wonderful. And some days are no fun at all! But no matter what kind of day you're having, God is always with you. So trust him. He will be there in the good times. And he will be there in the bad times too.

Love Note from God

**Don't be afraid.
I am with you.**

Isaiah 43:5

God Wants Us to Shine

DANIEL 6:1-23

Daniel loved God. He worked hard. He always did the right thing. And all the king's men hated him for it. So they set a trap. They tricked the king into signing their new law—*if you pray to God, you will be thrown into a den of hungry lions!*

The very next day, Daniel was caught praying to God. So the king's men threw Daniel in with the lions! The king was very upset. The next morning, he ran to the den! "Daniel, are you all right?" he cried.

"Yes!" Daniel replied. "God sent an angel to shut the lions' mouths." The king was so happy! He pulled Daniel out of the lions' den—and thanked God for keeping Daniel safe!

Love Note from Grandma

When you turn on a light, what happens? Darkness disappears! There's never a fight. Light wins every time. People might make fun of you for loving God. But don't give up! No matter what anyone says, keep trusting God. Be a shining light for him!

Love Note from God

Be a light for other people. . . .
Live so that they will praise
your Father in heaven.

Matthew 5:16

15

God's News Is Good News

JONAH 1–3

One day God said to Jonah, "Go to the great city of Nineveh. Tell the people there about my amazing love." But Jonah didn't want to go. He ran the other way! He hid in the bottom of a boat and fell fast asleep.

A terrible storm came up. Everyone was afraid the ship would sink! "It's all my fault," Jonah cried. "Throw me out. Then the storm will stop!" So out he went— *sploosh!*—down into the sea, *where he was swallowed by a huge fish!*

"Oh, Lord," Jonah prayed, "forgive me!" So the fish spat him out—*ptooo!* And the people of Nineveh heard about the amazing love of God.

Love Note from Grandma

God asks us to tell everyone about his amazing love. Some people might not want to hear it. But don't let that stop you. God's news is good news. So don't run away. And don't try to hide. Tell somebody the Good News about God's love!

16

Tell the Good News to everyone.

Mark 16:15

17

God Gives New Life

JOHN 3:1-17

There once was a man named Nicodemus. He was a good man who always obeyed the rules. He knew all about God. But his heart held a question that no one could answer—until he met Jesus.

"Master," Nicodemus whispered softly, "what must I do to get into heaven?"

"Nicodemus," Jesus replied, "unless you are born again, you cannot be in God's Kingdom. God loved the world so much that he gave his only Son, so that everyone who believes in him will never die. Anyone who loves and trusts in me will live with God in heaven *forever*."

Love Note from Grandma

Jesus loves you more than anything. He wants to be close to you forever. When you trust Jesus, he will fill your heart with new life. On that day you will be born again. And there will be a party in heaven!

18

If anyone belongs to Christ, then he is made new.

2 Corinthians 5:17

Jesus Loves Us

MARK 10:13-16

One day, as Jesus was speaking with his followers, a large crowd of little children came and gathered around them. Their parents wanted Jesus to pray for the children. But Jesus' followers became very angry. "Go away!" they shouted. "You're bothering Jesus!"

When Jesus heard this, his heart was very sad. "Do not stop them," Jesus said. "Let the little children come to me! God's Kingdom belongs to people who trust me like these little children do."

Then Jesus held the children in his arms and prayed for them. He asked God to bless them and fill their hearts with joy.

Love Note from Grandma

I will always love you. When you call me, I will answer you. When you need me, I will be there. You can come to me anytime. You can tell me anything. You are never bothering me. I love to be with you. That is my promise to you. And it's God's promise to you too— *forever.*

Love Note from God

This is how God showed his love to us: He sent his only Son into the world to give us life.

1 John 4:9

God Wants Us to Love Others

LUKE 10:30-35

One day a Jewish man set out on a journey. As he walked, he was attacked by robbers. They stole his money, beat him up, and left him to die. Soon a priest came by. But when the priest saw the man lying by the side of the road, he crossed over to the other side! Next came a man singing beautiful songs of praise. But he crossed the street as well. Wouldn't anybody help the poor man?

Finally a Samaritan walked by. Most Jews and Samaritans didn't like each other. But this Samaritan felt sorry for the Jewish man who was hurt. The Samaritan put medicine on his wounds, carried him to town, and found someone to care for him until he got better.

Love Note from Grandma

Jesus told us to love our neighbors. But what if our neighbors aren't very nice? Do we still have to love them? And what if they don't like us, but they need our help? What do we do then? That's right—we love and help them anyway.

Love Note from God

Anything you did for any of my people here, you also did for me.

Matthew 25:40

God Is Our Shepherd

LUKE 15:4-7

A very special shepherd had one hundred fluffy sheep. He loved all of them very much. One day one of his sheep wandered off. "Oh no!" he cried. "Where has she gone?"

The shepherd gathered up his other sheep. He put them in a safe place. Then he set off to find the one who was lost. When he found her, his heart was filled with joy! He carried her home with a thankful heart. Jesus loves us just like that. We are his sheep. He is our shepherd. He is so happy when we come back home to him.

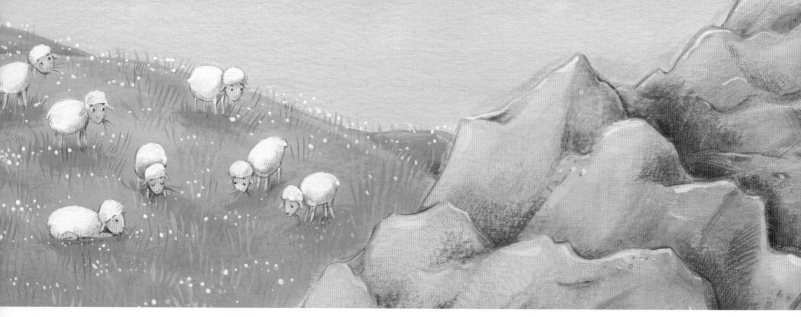

Love Note from Grandma

Did you ever lose something that you loved very much? It's hard to be happy until you find it. But oh, the joy when you do! Jesus knows when we are lost. He wants us back more than anything. And he won't stop looking until we're safe in his arms again.

Love Note from God

[Jesus] came to find lost people and save them.
Luke 19:10

God Forgives Our Mistakes

LUKE 15:11-24

A rich man had two sons. One day the younger son asked for some money. Then he packed his bags and left for a faraway country. There he wasted everything he had on wild parties and fancy things.

When his money was used up, the son began to starve! But no one would give him anything to eat. So he decided to go back home and ask for help. While he was still a long way off, his father saw him coming.

The father's heart was filled with joy. He ran to meet his son. "Bring my best robe—a ring and sandals, too! My son was lost. But now he is found!"

Love Note from Grandma

Everyone makes a few mistakes. But did you ever make a really bad mess—a mess so big you couldn't clean it up on your own? When we don't follow God's rules, we can make some big mistakes. Does that make God angry? No. He is waiting to forgive! So don't run away. Tell him what you've done. *God loves you.* When you ask him to forgive you, he always will.

Love Note from God

Happy are they whose sins are forgiven.

Romans 4:7

We Can Trust God

JOHN 11:1-44

"Lord, come quickly," the letter read. "Your friend Lazarus is very sick." But it was too late. When Jesus got to his friend's home, Lazarus had already been dead for four long days!

"Roll away the gravestone," Jesus told the people.

"But, Lord," Lazarus's sister cried, "the smell will be terrible!"

"Martha," Jesus whispered, "your brother will live again." Then he looked up to heaven, spread out his arms, and said, "Father, thank you for hearing me. I know you always hear me. Now, so everyone else will know you are God . . ."

Jesus turned toward Lazarus's tomb and shouted, "Lazarus—come out!"

And Lazarus did! He was alive again!

Love Note from Grandma

God is not in a hurry. His help always comes right on time. When God speaks, all of creation must obey. So tell him your problems. *Then trust him and wait.* When you learn to trust, God's answer will come!

Love Note from God

He who believes in me will have life even if he dies.

John 11:25

Jesus Is Alive!

MATTHEW 27:39-56; 28:5-7

Jesus was dying. "Come down from the cross, if you are really God's Son!" the crowd shouted.

"Father, forgive them," Jesus prayed.

"He saved others. Let him save himself!" the religious leaders spat. They were making fun of Jesus!

"Father, why have you forgotten about me?" Jesus asked.

"Maybe Elijah will help him come down!" an angry man said with a laugh.

"It is finished!" Jesus cried out. Then he took his last breath.

The sky turned black. The earth shook. The curtain in the Temple was torn in two.

"Surely he was the Son of God!" a soldier said as he fell to his knees.

Three days later, Mary stood before the empty tomb.

"He isn't dead anymore. He is risen!" she shouted. Her heart leaped with joy. *"Jesus is alive!"*

Love Note from Grandma

How much does Jesus love you? He loves you so much that he came down from heaven and became a man. He gave up being with God to become a person like you. Jesus lived a perfect life. He died on a cross. He came back to life again! And because he did, one day you can go up into heaven and be with him!

Love Note from God

I will be with you always.
Matthew 28:20

Visit Tyndale's website for kids at www.tyndale.com/kids.

TYNDALE is a registered trademark of Tyndale House Publishers, Inc. The Tyndale Kids logo is a trademark of Tyndale House Publishers, Inc.

My Time with Grandma Bible Storybook

Illustrated by Ela Jarzabek

Designed by Julie Chen

Edited by Brittany Buczynski

For manufacturing information regarding this product, please call 1-800-323-9400.

Library of Congress Cataloging-in-Publication Data

Smouse, Phil A.

  My time with grandma Bible storybook / by Phil Smouse ; illustrated by Ela Jarzabek.

    pages cm

  ISBN 978-1-4143-8318-7

1. Bible stories, English. 2. Children — Religious life — Juvenile literature. 3. Grandmothers — Religious life — Juvenile literature. 4. Grandparent and child — Religious aspects — Christianity — Juvenile literature. I. Jarzabek, Ela, illustrator. II. Title.

  BS551.3.S59 2013

  220.95'05 — dc23

2013006633

Printed in China

19	18	17	16	15	14	13
7	6	5	4	3	2	1